Essential Lives

ELEANOR ROOSEVELT

Essential Lives

ELEANOR ROOSEVELT

FIRST LADY & HUMAN RIGHTS ADVOCATE

by Katie Marsico

Content Consultant:
Victoria Grieve, Assistant Professor of History
Utah State University

ABDO
Publishing Company

CREDITS

Published by ABDO Publishing Company, 8000 West 78th Street,
Edina, Minnesota 55439. Copyright © 2008 by Abdo Consulting
Group, Inc. International copyrights reserved in all countries. No
part of this book may be reproduced in any form without written
permission from the publisher. The Essential Library™ is a
trademark and logo of ABDO Publishing Company.

Printed in the United States.

Editor: Jill Sherman
Copy Editor: Paula Lewis
Interior Design and Production: Rebecca Daum
Cover Design: Rebecca Daum

Library of Congress Cataloging-in-Publication Data
Marsico, Katie, 1980–
   Eleanor Roosevelt / Katie Marsico.
      p. cm. — (Essential lives)
   Includes bibliographical references.
   ISBN 978-1-60453-040-7
   1. Roosevelt, Eleanor, 1884-1962—Juvenile literature. 2.
Presidents' spouses—United States—Biography—Juvenile literature.
I. Title.

   E807.1.R48M28 2008
   973.917092—dc22
   [B]
                              2007030843

TABLE OF CONTENTS

Eleanor Roosevelt visits the Tuskegee Institute.

FLIGHT AT TUSKEGEE

On April 19, 1941, Eleanor Roosevelt was causing Secret Service agents to panic. The First Lady had been invited to tour the Tuskegee Army Air Field, in Tuskegee, Alabama. Eleanor was impressed by the all-African-American flying unit, the Ninety-ninth Pursuit Squadron, which was being trained there.

The wives of many former presidents preferred to spend their time organizing social gatherings in the White House. Eleanor was an exception. She was eager to know what was going on in her country and how she could help make it better. That often meant traveling outside the capital's borders. She would watch, listen, learn, and often share her observations with her husband, President Franklin Delano Roosevelt. On this trip, however, Eleanor was not content to simply look at airplanes and observe student drills. She was determined to take a plane ride with African-American flight instructor Charles A. Anderson.

STEPPING ONTO A PLANE AND TAKING A STAND

Anderson was an accomplished pilot, but even the most qualified African-American military personnel faced discrimination in the early 1940s. U.S. citizens of all races were willing to fight for the United States

Prevalent Discrimination

Prior to her famous flight with Anderson, Eleanor jokingly wondered aloud, "Can Negroes really fly airplanes?"[1] Anderson offered to let her see for herself, though the First Lady already knew the answer. Eleanor was not trying to insult the students or staff at Tuskegee. At the time, African Americans were experiencing widespread discrimination. Eleanor later became dedicated to fighting for equal rights for African Americans.

Tuskegee

African-American educator Booker T. Washington founded the Tuskegee Institute in 1881. The school focused on teaching African Americans farming and trade skills to help ensure their financial independence. Over time, however, the institute began offering a wide range of academic classes. It became the site of training programs for the U.S. Army Air Corps. The college has since been renamed Tuskegee University, and it instructs more than 3,000 students annually.

when war occurred. Segregation, however, prevented many African Americans from serving alongside white soldiers. Feelings of distrust and resentment often ruined what should have been a united effort against the enemy. Now Eleanor wanted to go up in a plane flown by an African American, and her team of white Secret Service agents could do little to stop her.

In a last-ditch effort to control the situation, agents phoned the president. After 36 years of marriage, however, Franklin knew his wife was fiercely determined and independent. If Eleanor insisted on flying with Anderson, it would take more than his staff to keep her on the ground.

Eleanor's plane ride not only resulted in a safe landing, but it also made a powerful statement about why segregation had no place on an airfield or in American society.

Tuskegee airmen make adjustments to a plane.

Eleanor returned to Franklin in Washington, D.C., with a photograph of her and Anderson on the plane. She was convinced that members of the ninety-ninth Pursuit Squadron possessed enough patriotism, courage, and talent to be used in the combat that would soon call Americans overseas.

The Tuskegee Airmen proved Eleanor right during World War II (1939–1945). Starting in May 1942, the Ninety-ninth Squadron was allowed to participate in missions in Europe and North Africa. They maintained an almost flawless record and—with the First Lady's help—demonstrated that African Americans were ready to serve their country. Eleanor was only too glad to have been of assistance. Though she came from a privileged background, Eleanor considered it her duty to aid

Proving Patriotism Is Color Blind

Eleanor realized that the country could not grow if discrimination continued in the United States. Eleanor was famous for her honest opinions and received letters from people around the world seeking her help and advice. During World War II, a soldier named Louis E. Chavis wrote Eleanor seeking her help for African-American troops who were being unfairly paid. The letter stated:

Mrs. Roosevelt ... since you are the only one that ... I believe will help us, as helpless colored soldiers striving to play our part in this war, will you please see that something is done for our benefit? ... May God ever continue to bless America and may it also be someday that we the Negro soldiers can enjoy some of America's freedom.[2]

Eleanor promptly wrote to Secretary of War Henry Stimson:

Over and over again, I have stressed the rights of every citizen ... I do not see how we can fight this war and deny these rights to any citizen in our own land.[3]

It would be several years before the U.S. government ended segregation in its armed forces. Even so, Eleanor played a part in reshaping the opinions of military leaders and politicians alike.

those who suffered from misfortune or oppression.

A Woman of Many Roles and Much Progress

Eleanor championed everyone from African-American troops to white families who lived in shacks and labored in sweatshops. She was more concerned about reaching out to other people than how people in society would judge her. She was not content to settle into the role of White House hostess and stay out of politics.

In an era when women were fighting for equal rights, Eleanor showed the world that it was possible for a wife and mother to also pursue a career, travel the globe, and bring about social change. Eleanor worked to that end before, during, and after her husband's presidency. She served on countless committees, visited faraway countries, and even

Relationship with the Tuskegee Institute

Eleanor's connection to the Tuskegee Institute did not end after her flight with Anderson. The school chose Cecil Peterson, a student, to correspond with the First Lady. Peterson wrote to Eleanor about his progress during training, and she responded with letters, candy, a book, and even a pair of track shoes.

Eleanor also kept in touch with the president of the Tuskegee Institute, F.D. Patterson. She welcomed Patterson to the White House in July 1941. They discussed the role of African Americans in aviation and national defense. Patterson was well aware of Eleanor's influence and often expressed his gratitude for her interest and support.

found time to write a newspaper column. No work was beneath her if it benefited someone else—she poured tea for kings and diplomats as First Lady and served coffee to wounded soldiers as a volunteer for the Red Cross.

During her 78 years of life, Eleanor made her mark as a homemaker, First Lady, proud American, philanthropist, and ambassador. As she later noted, "I could not, at any age, be content to take my place in a corner by the fireside and simply look on."[4]

Like many of her decisions, Eleanor's choice to fly over Tuskegee with Anderson unsettled some people, but it had a positive impact on millions more.

Air Travel

Eleanor's flight with Anderson certainly did not mark her first time in the sky. During the 1940s, many people still worried that air travel was risky. However, Eleanor often boarded planes to attend meetings or go on national and international tours. Pictures were often taken of her on or next to planes—Eleanor was a walking advertisement for the airline industry. Eleanor helped convince the public that flying was safe, fun, and convenient.

Eleanor poses with flight instructor Charles A. Anderson in his plane.

Eleanor, age three

A Childhood Filled with Challenges

Although Eleanor would one day be known as First Lady of the United States, her early life did not appear so promising. Anna Eleanor Roosevelt was born on October 11, 1884, in New York City. She was the first child of Anna Hall and Elliott Roosevelt. Both her parents came from wealthy families. Elliott was the younger brother of Theodore Roosevelt, who would serve as president of the United States from 1901 to 1909. Elliott's and Anna's distinguished backgrounds might have ensured a promising, comfortable home life for young Eleanor. However, her childhood was not always filled with love and laughter.

Anna and Elliott Roosevelt

Eleanor had a close relationship with her father, who nicknamed her Little Nell. Self-conscious and sensitive from a young age, she was able to forget some of her awkwardness in her father's presence. As Eleanor later recalled,

> I was a shy, solemn child even at the age of two, and I am sure that even when I danced I never smiled. … [My father] was the center of my world and all around him loved him.[1]

Unfortunately, Elliott frequently suffered from poor health and depression. This led him to drink and to abuse the drug morphine. These addictions hurt his health and strained his marriage to Anna.

Unlike her husband, Anna did not eagerly return Eleanor's affection. Anna was known for her beauty and elegance and was often cold toward her

Elliott Roosevelt

Before Elliott Roosevelt's alcoholism and depression became severe, he was a handsome, active man who enjoyed hunting, riding horses, and socializing. Unlike his brother Theodore—who attended Harvard College and entered politics—Elliott traveled around the world, including faraway countries such as India. After he and Anna married, they were popular in New York society and frequently gave and attended parties.

young daughter. As far as Anna was concerned, Eleanor was plain and awkward—two traits that led Anna to refer to the girl as Granny. The hurtful nickname devastated Eleanor, who already struggled with a lack of confidence.

Try as she might, Eleanor knew there was simply no pleasing Anna. Eleanor's mother was unhappy that Eleanor was not beautiful, and Eleanor was aware of these feelings. Anna tried to raise Eleanor so that her upbringing and manners would make up for her looks. Unfortunately, her mother's efforts only made young Eleanor more insecure about her appearance. Eleanor would never have the opportunity to learn if her relationship with her mother would change over time. Tragedy soon replaced the tension of her family life.

THE ROOSEVELT ORPHANS

Despite the couple's unhappy marriage, Anna and Elliott had two more children—Elliott Jr., born

Eleanor, second from right, with her father, Elliott, and brothers Hall and Elliott Jr.

in 1889, and Hall, born in 1891. As Elliott's troubles worsened, Anna kept busy by attending social engagements. She would also visit her mother, Mary Livingston Ludlow Hall, at her country home in Tivoli, New York. She and Elliott kept their distance from one another, and he was often separated from the family. Anna could do little to help her husband as he struggled to get better. Sadly, the two still had not reconciled by December 7, 1892, when Anna died from diphtheria.

While Eleanor grieved for her mother, the eight-year-old was also excited about the idea of a new life with her father. Elliott, however, was in no condition to care for three children. His problems only grew with Anna's passing. Eleanor and her brothers were sent to live with Grandmother Hall in New York City.

For Eleanor, the next two years were a time of difficult adjustments and tragedy. Grandmother Hall was a firm believer in discipline and education. Four aunts and uncles also shared her large home on Thirty-seventh Street. Eleanor, however, was most comfortable with the maids, butlers, and other household staff. Her father still came to visit, though it was clear that Anna's death had taken a toll on him. Little did he—or anyone else in the family—realize that they would soon be mourning again.

In early 1893, both Elliott Jr. and Hall became ill with scarlet fever. Hall recovered, but Elliott Jr. developed diphtheria and passed away. Overwhelmed by yet another family loss and already in poor

Charity

At the turn of the century, people who were wealthy and popular members of society were expected to be involved in charity work. Eleanor accompanied her adult relatives as they volunteered for various causes, including visiting and preparing meals for poor and crippled children. These charities made Eleanor aware that not everyone enjoyed a comfortable, privileged life as she did.

Eleanor in Long Island, New York, 1887

health, Eleanor's father died from a seizure on August 14, 1894. In less than two years, Eleanor had lost both of her parents and one of her brothers.

A New Life, No Questions Asked

So much death over so short a period of time was difficult for ten-year-old Eleanor to cope with.

Breaking the Rules

Young Eleanor quickly realized how much she loved books. However, even reading had rules in her grandmother's house. Generally, the children were allowed to read whatever they chose. But sometimes Eleanor noticed a book would mysteriously be lost if she asked too many questions or had a difficult time understanding it. Also, reading was only permitted during certain periods of the day. Eleanor, however, managed to find ways around some of these rules. As she later recalled, "I was not supposed to read in bed before breakfast, but as I [was] a self-willed child I used to hide a book under the mattress."[3]

She and her brother Hall continued to live with their grandmother in her homes in Tivoli, New York, and New York City. Though not unkind, Grandmother Hall was determined that the children obey her wishes at all times. Her decisions were not to be questioned. Even if they were questioned, she never gave a reason for her strict rules. As Eleanor later commented, "She so often said 'no' that I built up a defense of saying I did not want to do things in order to … keep down my disappointments."[2]

Under her grandmother's supervision, Eleanor spent her days sewing, learning French, playing the piano, and taking dance lessons. She also developed a love of reading and enjoyed seeing plays. A lonely child, Eleanor preferred the company of the household servants. She was particularly fond of a woman named Mrs. Overhalse who did the family's laundry. Sometimes Mrs. Overhalse let Eleanor help with the washing and ironing. This delighted Eleanor, who took great pleasure in feeling useful.

After her father's death, Eleanor saw little of the Roosevelts. She occasionally visited her uncle Theodore (whom she called "Ted") and his wife, Edith, at Sagamore House in Oyster Bay, New York. These trips were a relief from Eleanor's rigid lifestyle with Grandmother Hall. Uncle Ted often took Eleanor and her brother Hall camping or on picnics, and he encouraged them to play sports and listen to poetry readings. Eleanor had spent much of

Social Awareness

As an adult, Eleanor took up the cause of workers' rights and pushed for better treatment of women and child laborers. Looking back on her life at her grandmother's home on Thirty-seventh Street, she recalled the living conditions of the household staff:

[There were] inadequate servants' quarters ... which no one with any social conscience would tolerate today. ... The servants' room lacked ventilation and comfortable furnishings. Their bathroom was in the cellar, so each one had a basin and a pitcher in a tiny bedroom.[4]

She also marveled at how energetic and pleasant Mrs. Overhalse remained despite her countless responsibilities—all of which were performed without the help of modern machinery. Having become aware of the difficulties laborers faced, Eleanor emphasized that

Mrs. Overhalse was a cheerful, healthy soul, apparently able to direct her own household, come and wash all day for us, and then go back at night and finish up on her farm.[5]

Fashion

Once Eleanor was older, she did not look back fondly on the clothing she was forced to wear as a young girl. Her height and the popular styles of the day made her self-conscious. Her grandmother and aunts often dressed her in clothes that made her feel uncomfortable. Despite the fact that Eleanor was tall, they bought her clothes that better fit a shorter person. If she attended a party, the other girls had dresses that stretched halfway down their legs, while hers only reached above her knees.

her early life dealing with stress and sorrow. The vacations with Uncle Ted at Sagamore House offered her the much-needed opportunity to laugh, express herself, and build confidence.

After these brief visits to Sagamore House, Eleanor returned to her grandmother's care. By 1899, Grandmother Hall decided it was time to see one of her late daughter's wishes fulfilled—Eleanor should receive part of her schooling in Europe. In the autumn of 1899, the 15-year-old prepared to cross the Atlantic Ocean and continue her education at Allenswood School near London, England. ⌐

Eleanor's school portrait, 1898

Allenswood School in England, 1900

Eager for
Social Change

Life at Allenswood School was not without
rules and discipline, but Eleanor quickly
discovered that she admired and respected the
French headmistress, Mademoiselle Marie Souvestre.
Eleanor became one of Mademoiselle Souvestre's

favorite students and was often invited to spend evenings in her private study. Madame Souvestre read poetry, plays, and stories. With the headmistress's help, Eleanor became more comfortable at her new school. She gained the acceptance she never had back home.

Eleanor had several opportunities to travel while attending Allenswood. In 1902, she began to accompany Mademoiselle Souvestre on her journeys across Europe. As Eleanor later wrote,

> *This was one of the most momentous things that happened in my education. … Traveling with Mademoiselle Souvestre was a revelation. She did all the things that in a vague way you had always felt you wanted to do.*[1]

In addition to visiting interesting locations, Eleanor also gained valuable self-confidence. She was put in charge of making all the travel

Gaining Confidence

While at Allenswood, Eleanor journeyed with Mademoiselle Souvestre through England, France, Switzerland, Germany, Italy, and Belgium. Besides adding to her pupil's confidence, Mademoiselle Souvestre taught Eleanor how to be spontaneous and to appreciate adventure. At the last minute, the French headmistress would suddenly change their schedule to visit a friend or enjoy a day at the beach. Her travels with Mademoiselle Souvestre helped Eleanor become less rigid and more open to new experiences.

arrangements. It was both flattering and encouraging that a wise, older woman such as Mademoiselle Souvestre trusted a 16-year-old girl with these responsibilities.

A Bad Habit or an Invaluable Trick?

During her early years at Allenswood, Eleanor developed what she believed to be a bad habit of introducing topics she knew little about in conversation. Eleanor often found herself sitting across from Mademoiselle Souvestre at the dinner table. Eleanor struggled with conversation and began mentioning topics she had overheard the teacher discuss with her friends. Mademoiselle Souvestre was impressed with her interest and happily did all the talking. In the process, Eleanor learned a great deal about whatever topic she had brought up. This trick served her well in the years to come:

> More and more, as I grew older, I used the quickness of my mind to pick the minds of other people and use their knowledge as my own. A dinner companion, a casual acquaintance, provided me with information which I could [later] use in conversation.[2]

Eleanor wrote that she considered this to be a bad habit. After all, she did not want to be caught pretending to be more educated about a subject than she actually was. Still, it helped her learn. Eleanor later admitted that her habit actually helped her because she was introduced to a wide variety of subjects she might never have learned about.

RETURN TO NEW YORK

Eleanor finished her education at Allenswood in 1902. She was deeply saddened to be leaving her mentor. Nonetheless, she returned to the United States a much different person. The shy, nervous student who had arrived three years earlier was gone. The new Eleanor had discovered that she was a useful, valuable young woman. She could contribute to intelligent conversations as well as learn from them. She finally felt capable of making friends and thinking and acting independently. These skills would be important once she returned to New York. Eleanor was 18 years old and it was time to make her social debut.

Eleanor was not eager to return to her old life in New York. She had gained self-esteem abroad, but attending frequent social engagements proved stressful. After having been away at school, Eleanor was forced to reacquaint herself with people she had not seen in years. Also, the idea of making small talk with young men she had never met put her newfound confidence to the test.

Occasionally, Eleanor recognized a familiar face at the endless events and introductions. Eleanor's distant cousin Franklin would sometimes appear at a

An Independent Woman

Like so many young ladies from socially elite families, Eleanor was not expected to pursue a career after she finished her education. Her main duty was to find a successful husband. In the meantime, she still needed money and a place to live. At first, she stayed at her grandmother's houses in Tivoli and New York City. By 1903, however, she was living with Susie Parish, one of her many distant cousins. She received an allowance between $5,000 and $8,000 each year from Grandmother Hall. Susie's husband taught her to keep track of her expenses and use her money wisely.

*Franklin D. Roosevelt and Eleanor Roosevelt
in Campobello, New York, 1904*

party or on a train trip to Tivoli. His parents, James
and Sara Delano Roosevelt, had enjoyed a friendly
relationship with her parents. As time passed, it
became clear that Eleanor and Franklin would also
be close.

There was no denying that there were some striking differences between them. Eleanor was often shy and somber, tall for her age, and considered plain looking. By comparison, Franklin was handsome, charming, and had a talent for socializing and telling jokes. He easily fit the role of a future politician.

> "Do what you feel in your heart to be right—for you'll be criticized anyway. You'll be damned if you do, and damned if you don't."[3]
>
> —*Eleanor Roosevelt*

Despite what they did not have in common, Franklin wanted to get to know Eleanor better. He was especially interested in her efforts with the poor. Young women entering society were expected to do charity work. But Eleanor did not view her visits to some of New York City's poorest neighborhoods as a required duty. She always was eager to be useful, and she found her charity work to be rewarding. She also recognized that her help was desperately needed by residents of Rivington Street on the city's Lower East Side.

ANOTHER SIDE OF LIFE IN THE UNITED STATES

By the early 1900s, New York City was a perfect example of why the United States was becoming known as a melting pot. People from vastly different

cultures, religions, races, and economic backgrounds
called New York City home. But the world Eleanor
knew best was filled with elegant functions and
private educations. It was completely different
from the lives the residents living in New York's
Lower East Side faced. The area was filled with poor
immigrants. They often labored long, hard hours in
local factories. These jobs barely paid enough to feed
their families. They were forced to live in run-down,
overcrowded apartments known as tenement houses.
In these homes, basic necessities such as heat and
water often were unavailable. Many children were
not able to attend school because they had to work
and help their families survive.

Eleanor got a firsthand look at this desperate
situation when she joined the Junior League
in 1903. Created just two years earlier, the
organization's goal was to improve struggling
communities, such as New York's Lower East Side.
As a volunteer, Eleanor spent her time teaching local
children at the Rivington Street Settlement House.

That same year, Eleanor joined the National
Consumers League. She was asked to investigate
working conditions in garment factories and
department stores. Her work made her aware of the

challenges many women faced in their jobs. As she admitted,

> It had never occurred to me that the girls might get tired standing behind counters all day long, or that no seats were provided for them if they had time to sit down and rest. [4]

As an investigator, Eleanor learned firsthand about the United States' sweatshops. People of all ages labored with little light, fresh air, or guarantee of personal safety. Fires often broke out in these dismal factories. It was not unusual for the working poor to pay with their lives.

Eleanor's work opened her eyes to the poverty that many Americans faced. Until this time, Eleanor was relatively unaware of just how bad it was in the poor neighborhoods of New York. After a while, she began to ask Franklin to join her on her visits to the Lower East Side. At the time, Franklin was a senior at Harvard

Tenement Houses

When immigrants first arrived in the United States, they often had little money, large families, and were in desperate need of homes. Rent in tenement houses on New York City's Lower East Side was cheap, but the houses were rundown.

Today, the Lower East Side Tenement Museum is located in what was formerly a tenement house in the 1860s. The overcrowded building was designed to accommodate four families on each of the five floors. Seven people often occupied a three-room apartment and shared a bedroom, a living room, and a kitchen.

College in Cambridge, Massachusetts. He was as shocked by the poverty and suffering as Eleanor had been. It was a side of the United States that he had never seen so closely.

Franklin and Eleanor were beginning a pattern that would follow them through the rest of their lives. Eleanor often opened Franklin's eyes to various social injustices. Together they tried to do whatever they could to correct it. After being exposed to life in New York City slums, the pair would continue to dedicate their lives to the fight against poverty and for the rights of the working class.

Franklin began thinking about Eleanor more and more. Eleanor was an educated and intelligent woman. More importantly, Franklin saw she was a compassionate human being who wanted to improve people's lives and who had the makings of an excellent wife and mother.

New York tenement building

Eleanor married Franklin on March 17, 1905.

STARTING A FAMILY

y the autumn of 1903, Franklin had proposed marriage to Eleanor, and she had accepted. Their courtship was brief but not uncommon for those days. Romance was quite formal and generally did not include many outward expressions of affection. Often, a young couple only exchanged polite correspondence and rarely held hands until they were engaged. In many ways, marriage in the early 1900s was merely the next step in a young woman's life. As Eleanor admitted,

> *I had high standards of what a wife and mother should be and not the faintest notion of what it meant to be either a wife or mother, and none of my elders enlightened me.*[1]

Setting the Date

Eleanor and Franklin's wedding date—March 17—was selected for several reasons. First, it was Eleanor's late mother's birthday. Secondly, it was Saint Patrick's Day and New York City was hosting a large parade, which President Theodore Roosevelt was planning to attend. Since Eleanor's Uncle Ted was a busy man, it would be easier for him to attend on a day he would already be in town.

Perhaps sensing the couple's naiveté—or wishing that Franklin would pick a more glamorous wife—Franklin's mother, Sara, tried to stall the marriage. She encouraged the couple to wait to announce their engagement. She even sent her son on a cruise to the West Indies, hoping that some time away would change his mind.

Sara Roosevelt's plans failed. By the fall of 1904, Franklin was a law student at Columbia University in New York City, and the world knew that he and Eleanor were officially engaged.

A Blushing Bride and a Society Matron

On March 17, 1905, Eleanor and Franklin were married in an elegant wedding. Everyone dressed in the most stylish fashions. The bride wore a long satin gown and carried a bouquet of lilies of the valley. Uncle Ted, then four years into his presidency, gave Eleanor away. Guests had to push through dense crowds of curious onlookers and traffic to make it into the ceremony. The ceremony was held in the adjoining homes of Eleanor's second cousin, Susie Parish, and Susie's mother.

Afterward, the newlyweds enjoyed a short honeymoon at the Roosevelts' estate in Hyde Park, New York, where they eventually moved in the summer of 1905. Once Franklin finished law school for the year, he and Eleanor were finally able to enjoy a more glamorous vacation in Europe. When they returned to New York, they moved into a house Franklin's mother had purchased for them at 125 East Thirty-sixth Street, three blocks from her own home.

Sara had already selected furniture and hired servants. Eleanor's main job was to become more social, less shy, and start thinking about a family. As a young wife and mother, Eleanor relied heavily on the servants to help her with the duties of running a house. During this period, she devoted much of her time to activities typical of a society matron in the early 1900s. She knitted, read, hosted dinners, and took lessons in French, German, and Italian. Eleanor later regretted having servants during those early years of her marriage. She realized that there was knowledge and self-confidence to be gained by taking control of the housework and the children.

NEW FAMILY, NEW RELATIONSHIPS

On May 3, 1906, Franklin and Eleanor welcomed their first child,

A Minor Distraction

The *New York Times* published an article about the marriage ceremony on March 18, 1905. The Roosevelt family was prominent in New York City's social scene and in national politics. It was not surprising that major newspapers took interest:

One of the most notable weddings of the year was that celebrated yesterday, when Miss Eleanor Roosevelt, daughter of the only brother of President (Theodore) Roosevelt, and Franklin Delano Roosevelt, a cousin of the president, were married.[2]

A large part of the excitement was due to the attendance of her Uncle Ted. Eleanor later commented:

Those closest to us did take time to wish us well, but the great majority of the guests were more interested in being able to see and listen to the President—and in a short time this young married couple were standing alone![3]

The attention Uncle Ted received upset neither Eleanor nor her new husband. They enjoyed listening to the president's stories just as much as their guests.

Franklin and Eleanor Roosevelt in Hyde Park, New York

Anna. A son named James was born in 1907.
Eleanor was frequently ill, tired, and forced to divide
her schedule between her children and her many
social obligations. She found herself becoming more

dependent on her mother-in-law's decisions, a fact that did not always please Eleanor.

Eleanor once said of her relationship with Sara,

[I] never thought of asking for anything that ... would not meet with her approval. She was a very strong character ... She was somewhat jealous of anything that might mean a really deep attachment outside the family circle.[4]

Eleanor did not always appreciate Sara's influence to control family life. They often disagreed on issues of parenting. Though Eleanor was truly grateful for all that Sara had done for them—and even for some of the decisions she had made for them—she also longed for a little independence.

In the end, Sara often won out. Franklin usually did not see anything wrong with letting his mother have her way. In 1908, he and Eleanor moved to a new house at 49 East Sixty-fifth Street. Sara had insisted the growing family needed more space, and she even bought the home next door for herself.

At first, Eleanor was completely miserable in the house on East Sixty-fifth Street. Much to Franklin's alarm, she sat down at her dressing table one day and began sobbing. She later recounted the reason for her sadness:

Franklin, Sara, and Eleanor Roosevelt in Newburgh, New York.
Sara was a constant presence in the young couple's life.

I did not like to live in a house which was not in any way

mine, one that I had done nothing about and which did not

represent the way I wanted to live. ... I was not developing any individual taste or initiative. I was simply absorbing the personalities of those about me and letting their tastes and interests dominate me.[5]

Despite Eleanor's uneasy relationship with Sara, she was soon forced to cope with far more distressing issues.

On March 18, 1909, Eleanor gave birth to Franklin Jr. Eleanor was thrilled to have another child. Tragically, Franklin Jr. lived less than eight months. In November, the infant died from influenza, a flu that was often fatal in the early 1900s. Eleanor was grief stricken, but eventually she resumed her duties as a wife and mother.

The birth of their son, Elliott, in September 1910 helped ease some of the family's sorrow. While the previous year had dragged on for Eleanor as she struggled to overcome the pain of her child's death, life was

First Inauguration

After marrying Franklin, Eleanor was greatly exposed to national politics. She had, however, visited the White House long before she became First Lady. Eleanor attended her Uncle Ted's inauguration in Washington, D.C., on March 4, 1905. Eleanor later confessed that although she was thrilled to be present, her mind was more focused on the event than on her uncle's plans for the country.

suddenly busier than ever. Franklin had left his job
at a local law firm and was campaigning for a seat
in the New York Senate. With this introduction to
politics, he began a public career that would change
the United States. Although Eleanor may not have
known it in 1910, she would shortly do the same. ⌣

Eleanor, James, Anna, and Franklin Roosevelt pose for a family portrait in 1908.

Eleanor Roosevelt, 1915

MORE THAN A
POLITICIAN'S WIFE

*I*t appeared that Franklin had a knack for politics right from the start. The race for a seat in the New York Senate was not an easy one. Franklin was nominated by the Democrats in Dutchess County, an area that favored Republicans.

But Franklin was determined. He tirelessly visited even the smallest villages, chatting with local farmers and listening to the concerns and opinions of the people. His efforts with the voters paid off, and he began work as a state senator on January 1, 1911.

Initially, Eleanor kept busy caring for her growing family and organizing their new home in Albany, New York. As time passed, her outlook and ambitions began to change. Without her mother-in-law's constant presence and with Franklin busy in the New York Senate, Eleanor was forced to become independent. In Albany, Eleanor recommitted herself to public service. She felt this was her duty whether or not Franklin was in office.

By 1912, Franklin was working to be reelected to the state senate, but he became ill with a fever. Unable to campaign, he relied on political

Foreign Languages

As a political wife, Eleanor often found that her familiarity with other languages came in handy. At state events where diplomats from various nations were present, she sometimes was able to carry on a discussion more skillfully than Franklin.

At one function, she conversed easily with guests who sat on either side of her at the dinner table, despite the fact that one of the languages being spoken was French. Franklin, however, struggled to make small talk with the woman on his right, who only knew Spanish. Eleanor humorously noted that he simply repeated the same question over and over as the evening wore on. "All he could say was: 'How many children have you, madam?' to which she always responded smilingly with the number and nothing more!"[1]

adviser Louis Howe, who helped him win reelection. With Eleanor's support, Franklin furthered his career in politics. In 1913, he and Eleanor moved to Washington, D.C., after President Woodrow Wilson appointed him assistant secretary of the Navy.

A Nation at War

Once in the nation's capital, Eleanor quickly understood that Franklin's busy career increased her own duties and obligations. The birth of two more children—Franklin Jr. in 1914 and John in 1916—added to her responsibilities. She was also expected to pay social visits to other politicians' wives. Eleanor's schedule grew so full that she soon hired a personal secretary.

Life became more hectic when World War I (1914–1918) erupted. At first, the United States had limited involvement, but by 1917, the United States had joined the conflict. Franklin's job suddenly required even more of his time and attention.

Finding Balance

Once the United States entered World War I, Eleanor had to balance her careers as a homemaker, political wife, and public servant.

Occasionally, Eleanor's many duties overlapped. Sometimes she would race home from the canteen in her Red Cross uniform just as dinner guests were arriving at the front door. She later commented that, even if such instances caused her to panic, at least they taught her how to change clothes quickly.

Eleanor volunteered to work with the Red Cross—an organization dedicated to helping the sick or wounded during war or disaster. Much of her effort centered on the Red Cross canteen, a recreation area where soldiers could enjoy a meal and a conversation. Eleanor's duties included talking to troops, preparing food, and cleaning up. In her spare time, she helped found the Navy Red Cross, which knitted wool socks to be sent to American forces overseas.

Eleanor also visited veterans at Saint Elizabeth's Hospital. Many of the men were seriously injured and deeply disturbed by their war experiences. She was horrified by the lack of attention some patients received. She wrote Franklin Lane, secretary of the interior, urging him to investigate patient care. Instances like this during World War I changed Eleanor. She became more confident and determined to correct social injustices. Eleanor once said:

> *I became a more tolerant person. I had gained some assurance about my ability to run things and the knowledge that there is joy in accomplishing a good job. I knew more about the human heart.* [2]

The Roosevelt family was living in Washington, D.C., in 1918.

STRENGTHENING OF CHARACTER

Despite Eleanor's knowledge of human character and emotions, her own heart was about to be broken. She was devastated in 1918 when she discovered that Franklin was romantically involved with her secretary. Eleanor offered him a divorce, which both he and his mother refused. They argued that a divorce would hurt Franklin's political career. Instead, he promised to end the romantic relationship.

The following years intensified Eleanor's personal struggles. Grandmother Hall died in August 1919, which added to the somber atmosphere at home. In 1920, Franklin lost the vice presidency with presidential candidate James Cox. No matter what personal sadness or frustration she was feeling, Eleanor continued to be dedicated to public service.

The Right to Vote

Though Eleanor eventually became well-known in the crusade for women's rights, she initially did not have strong feelings about a woman's right to vote. When Franklin first became involved in politics she admitted, "I had never given the question serious thought, for I took it for granted that men were superior creatures and knew more about politics than women did. ... I cannot claim to have been a feminist in those early days."[3]

Eleanor had not forgotten the plight of women and child laborers. She served with representatives from other countries at the International Congress of Working Women (ICWW) and joined the League of Women Voters (LWV) in 1920. That same year the Nineteenth Amendment was ratified, giving women the right to vote. Eleanor was asked to report to the league about national legislation in Washington, D.C. The LWV's goal was to educate citizens— especially women—about political issues that their votes could now influence.

She later recalled how her public service efforts during this period helped her discover her own personality and all that she was capable of:

> *I was thinking things out for myself and becoming an individual. Had I never done this, perhaps I might have been saved some difficult experiences, but I have never regretted even my mistakes. They all added to my understanding of other human beings, and I came out in the end a more ... understanding and charitable person.* [4]

New Political Horizons

After Franklin's 1920 defeat as a vice presidential candidate, he resumed practicing law. The family once again spent much of their time in New York. When their schedules allowed, the Roosevelts took trips to their summer home on Campobello Island in New Brunswick, Canada. In August 1921, one of these vacations proved life changing. Franklin became ill and was diagnosed with polio, an infection that affected his nervous system and left his legs paralyzed. He began therapy and was able to move with the help of crutches or a wheelchair. Still, the sickness was a harsh blow to the once robust Franklin and all those around him.

Regardless of how much his mother disagreed, Eleanor, Howe, and Franklin's doctor encouraged him to lead an active and normal lifestyle. Back in New York, he took a job at an insurance company, and Eleanor continued her work with women's rights organizations. In 1922, she became a member of the Women's Trade Union League (WTUL), which helped create better pay and improved working conditions for women in the workforce. She also spoke at luncheons and raised funds for the women's division of the Democratic State Committee. In 1926, Eleanor and two of her friends purchased

A House with Happy Memories

Despite the fact that Franklin suffered the onset of polio at Campobello, neither he nor Eleanor lost their affection for the Canadian island. Sara Delano Roosevelt bought them a furnished house there in 1909. The Roosevelt Cottage, as it is often called, sits on 5 acres (2 ha) of land and features 34 rooms, 76 windows, and 7 fireplaces.

Franklin and Eleanor regularly vacationed at the cottage from 1909 until 1921. When they were not fishing, sailing, or swimming, they entertained guests who also appreciated Campobello's seaside beauty. Once national politics consumed more of their time, it became more difficult to visit so often.

Eleanor began working on her memoirs at Campobello in 1935 and opened the cottage to a student leadership institute in the early 1940s. In 1962, she made her final trip to Campobello for the dedication of the Franklin Delano Roosevelt Memorial Bridge, which connects the island to Lubec, Maine. Regardless of the trauma Eleanor experienced there in 1921, she always looked fondly upon their Campobello home.

the Todhunter School for girls in New York City. She taught several subjects, including classes in literature, history, and current events.

These activities brought her into the public spotlight. Howe gave her advice on delivering speeches and kept her informed about the different angles of various political issues. Eleanor grew more confident and people began to see her as a woman of influence both in social reform and in her relationship with Franklin.

When she attended the New York State Democratic Convention in 1928, local politicians asked her to encourage her husband to run for governor. Eleanor firmly replied that she would not force Franklin—who was still undergoing physical therapy—to do anything he did not want to. Ultimately, Franklin accepted the nomination and won the governorship that year. By 1929, the Roosevelts returned to Albany and once more prepared to serve their country.

Hard Times

Eleanor and Franklin returned to New York after he was diagnosed with polio. Life was stressful. Servants, immediate family, and others were packed into his mother's home—including Howe and a trained nurse. Tensions ran high on subjects ranging from Franklin's care to who should have the largest room. Eleanor would look back on that time as the most difficult winter of her life.

Eleanor and Franklin returned to New York by 1922.

Franklin and Eleanor Roosevelt in the White House

Paving the Way to the White House

Eleanor was used to her husband holding public office during the nation's difficult times. After all, Franklin had been involved in national politics during World War I. He had a great deal of experience dealing with crises. The

new governor of New York took office at a moment
when the country was about to enter one of its most
tumultuous eras—the Great Depression.

Before Franklin began his term as governor,
the United States was growing more and more
prosperous. Business owners and manufacturers
enjoyed great success. People who wanted a
taste of the wealth invested in the stock market.
Unfortunately, many people had to borrow money to
purchase stocks. It was a risk, but there was no reason
to think that the prosperity that the United States was
experiencing would soon end.

On October 24, 1929, stock prices suddenly
dropped. Investors panicked. They wanted to sell off
their stocks as quickly as possible, even if it meant
selling them for less than the purchase price. Within
days, the stock market had crashed. Americans
confidence in the economy faltered. Over the next
few years businesses ranging from farms to banks to
factories began to fail. Americans were left out of
work, poor, homeless, and in an economic crisis that
challenged the most skilled politicians.

Both Eleanor and Franklin were deeply moved
by the suffering around them. Families could not
afford to feed their children. Education was not a

priority for those who did not know when they would get their next meal. President Herbert Hoover tried to help the nation recover. However, Hoover did not strongly favor government programs for relief efforts. He believed that Americans would be able to turn things around for themselves. Unfortunately, the United States' economic depression only worsened. Over the next three years, other countries began to feel the backlash of the United States' economic troubles.

Frustrated by the lack of progress, Franklin decided to push for a stronger voice in national government. As Eleanor recalled,

[He had] a conviction that the depression could be licked. ...

Giving Hope to America's Youth

One of Eleanor's main concerns was how the Great Depression affected children and teenagers. She understood that the country's economic crisis made young people feel angry, frustrated, and hopeless. Eleanor pushed Franklin to establish the New Deal program that would aid unemployed youth in the United States.

The National Youth Administration (NYA) was founded in 1935 to help pay tuition for students who participated in work study programs at their high schools and colleges. The NYA also offered training to teenagers who sought employment with government-funded projects.

In 1937, educator and social activist Mary McLeod Bethune was asked to run a special branch of the NYA for African-American youth. People of all races suffered the financial hardships of the Great Depression, but African Americans also had to cope with discrimination when seeking education or applying for jobs.

The thing he felt most strongly was that there was a vitality in the people that could be salvaged.[1]

With this in mind, Franklin decided to run for president in 1932. Though Eleanor was reluctant about her husband's latest political goal, she gave him her support and watched as he told voters how he would lead the country out of crisis.

A Future in the White House

Eleanor was worried about Franklin's campaign for the presidency. Eleanor was happy in New York, where she spent her time teaching. She also had started a furniture business with two friends called Val-Kill Industries. She later admitted,

For myself, I was deeply troubled. As I saw it, this meant the end of any personal life of my own. ... I had recently enjoyed a certain amount

Christmas Volunteer

Eleanor rarely took a break from her volunteer work—even on Christmas Eve. She often spent that day going to parties for underprivileged children and giving out food baskets to the needy. On one occasion, Eleanor sang Christmas carols to those living in the poorest neighborhoods of Washington, D.C.

*of ... independence and had been able to do things in which I
was personally interested.*[2]

Eleanor was concerned about the prospect of
life in the White House. As the governor's wife, she
had accompanied Franklin on inspections of state
hospitals and prisons. These experiences helped her
learn more about public service and the standards
to which social institutions should be held. But as
First Lady, she would always be in the public eye.
Eleanor worried that she would have more formal
responsibilities and fewer opportunities to pursue
the work she really wanted to do.

Franklin won over the people. His campaigning,
which included extensive traveling and radio
broadcasts, convinced Americans that he was
determined to pull them out of the Great
Depression. On March 4, 1933, Franklin Delano
Roosevelt was sworn in as the thirty-second president
of the United States.

Franklin had to live up to huge expectations. He
had promised relief from poverty, frustration, and
hopelessness in a nation where approximately 15
million citizens were out of work. The public looked
to him to keep his word. Franklin immediately

pushed to put his New Deal programs into effect. The New Deal included several government-funded acts and agencies that provided jobs and helped reshape the economy.

His programs included the Public Works Administration (PWA) and the Civil Works Administration (CWA). These programs gave the unemployed opportunities to earn money constructing buildings, bridges, dams, airports, and highways. The Agricultural Adjustment Act (AAA) helped stabilize the value of farmers' crops. The Civilian Conservation Corps (CCC) gave young men jobs caring for the country's natural resources. Eleanor did her part to support New Deal policies. The early part of Franklin's presidency proved to Eleanor that her role as First Lady would not limit her ability to promote social causes.

Duty of the First Lady

At first, Eleanor did not appreciate all of her new responsibilities as First Lady. As the months passed, however, she began to view those duties differently. She later said, "To many people the White House symbolizes the government, and though standing and shaking hands for an hour or so, two or three times a week, is not an inspiring occupation, still I think it well worth while."[3]

Eleanor supported Franklin's New Deal programs.

Playing a Role in the Country's Recovery

Once it became apparent that the new First Lady was committed to making a difference, letters poured into Washington, D.C. Many of the writers pleaded for help in the form of money or clothing. Others expressed their admiration.

My Dear Mrs. Roosevelt—mother of our country ... I am writing you a letter to ... help my poor boy ... with the depression he lost all he had.[4]

Dear Madam ... I am a poor mother with ten children ... and I have no way of making a living.[5]

Dear Mrs. Roosevelt ... It is inspiring to know we have as our "first lady," one so really great and influential, who is so kindhearted—charmingly simple and wholly unselfish.[6]

Even if Eleanor could not help every American who contacted her during the Great Depression, she tried her best to respond or to offer advice.

She lent extra support to certain New Deal programs, including the Arthurdale Subsistence Homestead Project in West Virginia. This project was intended to be a newly constructed community for poor laborers. The concept was that

Letters

Eleanor did not just receive letters from adults during the Great Depression. Children often wrote her, too, and asked for everything from money and dolls to bicycles and football shoes. Some children even begged for her used clothes so they would have something to wear to school.

Eleanor visits the Arthurdale Subsistence Homestead Project in West Virginia.

residents would farm the land, develop small businesses, and escape poverty. Eleanor worked with Secretary of the Interior Harold Ickes to make sure that Arthurdale would not become another run-down slum. She pushed for well-built houses with indoor plumbing and insulation to prevent heat loss in winter.

Eleanor also spoke out against discrimination based on race or gender. Sometimes, she gave radio broadcasts, public speeches, and press conferences that were open only to women reporters. These press conferences helped ensure the position of female reporters, as they were guaranteed a good story that their male counterparts did not have access to. By 1935, she had her own newspaper column, "My Day." Eleanor wrote this column six days a week. In it, she discussed topics from political issues to popular plays.

Despite her agenda, Eleanor still devoted time as the hostess of the White House. She presided over state dinners and entertained visiting diplomats. As Franklin prepared to campaign for reelection in 1936, it seemed clear that he stood an excellent chance of winning.

Campaigning

When the 1936 presidential race was underway, Eleanor occasionally visited campaign headquarters or traveled with Franklin as he spoke to voters around the country. Though she contributed to several political and social reforms as First Lady, she preferred not to actively participate in Franklin's campaign efforts.

Something else was clear: Eleanor had become a powerful voice in politics as an advocate for social reform. She viewed her role as First Lady as a tool for change. The public was growing aware of this, as was the president. As Eleanor recalled,

> *Franklin often used me to get the reflection of other people's thinking because he knew I made it a point to see and talk with a variety of people. [He] knew that I would not be satisfied to be merely an official hostess.*[7]

Eleanor serves soup at the Grand Central Restaurant in New York City during the Great Depression.

Eleanor votes in the 1936 election.

UNAFRAID TO MAKE WAVES

By the time Franklin was reelected in 1936, the general feeling that Eleanor shared with much of the public was that the country was just starting to get back on its feet. Franklin had developed successful programs and policies that helped the United States recover financially, though the country would not fully recover for years. And as far as Eleanor was concerned, not all of the nation's problems were related to money.

Eleanor had realized that African Americans were often treated unfairly even before she became First Lady. During Franklin's first term of office, however, Eleanor learned that segregation often was accepted by the government. This became apparent when she supported antilynching legislation. The proposed bill would outlaw the violence that often claimed the lives of African Americans in the South.

Franklin agreed with the ideas behind the bill, but he was worried about offending Southern politicians. Eleanor, however, simply pushed harder and harder on behalf of the National Association for the Advancement of Colored People (NAACP). In response, Franklin and members of his staff became frustrated and unwilling to listen to her argument. She responded by attending an NAACP-sponsored art exhibit called A Commentary on Lynching. Her actions shocked and enraged people who had not accepted racial equality.

In the end, the law was not passed. Eleanor did not give up her fight to end racism and segregation, even if her beliefs were not always popular.

By Franklin's second term, she found new opportunities to fight discrimination. In February 1939, she resigned from the Daughters of the American Revolution (DAR), a women's volunteer group that promoted American independence and patriotism. The DAR refused to let African-American opera singer Marion Anderson perform in their concert hall in Washington, D.C. Anderson had performed for the Roosevelts at the White House in 1936 and again in 1938, and Eleanor was aware of her talent.

Upon hearing of the DAR's unwelcoming attitude, she submitted her letter of resignation in the following terms:

I am in complete disagreement with the attitude taken in refusing ... a great artist. You had an opportunity to lead in an enlightened way and it seems to me your organization has failed.[1]

Unpopular Actions

In 1936, Eleanor hosted a garden party at the White House for girls who attended a local reform school. Some of the students were African American. This fact concerned Franklin's political advisers and earned the First Lady harsh words from Southern newspapers. Despite their reactions, the president neither questioned nor criticized his wife. Though some of Eleanor's actions were unpopular, they did not jeopardize Franklin's role as president.

News of her decision made headlines across the country and Eleanor mentioned it in her "My Day" column. She even arranged for Anderson to perform at the Lincoln Memorial. It was clear that the First Lady refused to accept social injustice from anyone.

Eleanor also continued to crusade for better treatment of women in the workforce. Franklin's second term as president occurred at a time when the country was only just beginning to recover from the Great Depression. In Eleanor's opinion, women deserved to be a part of that progress. They should have the opportunity to hold jobs and make money. Eleanor earned an income from writing her column and books, as well as from speaking at lectures and on the radio. When the United States became involved in a second world war, women proved the wisdom behind Eleanor's request as they took over the jobs left by men sent to fight overseas.

Empress Eleanor?

Once a shy little girl unsure of her place in life, it seemed that Eleanor had become a different person. But was the First Lady supposed to be so outspoken and take such an active interest in politics? How much influence did "Empress Eleanor," as some of her critics had begun to call her, have over the president? According to Eleanor, her influence was not as great as everyone assumed.

Eleanor explained,

> While I often felt strongly on various subjects, Franklin frequently refrained from supporting causes in which he believed, because of political realities. There were times when this annoyed me very much.[2]

Eleanor continued to state her mind, and she independently pursued changes that she considered socially important:

> As time went by, I found that people no longer considered me a mouthpiece for my husband but realized that I had a point of view of my own with which he might not at all agree. … Franklin himself never tried to discourage me and was undisturbed by anything I wanted to say or do.[3]

Franklin's advisers, however, worried about Eleanor's bold attitude and powerful convictions. Not only did she want to end segregation—she also promoted women taking a more active voice in politics and gaining equality in the workplace. She even approached Washington, D.C., officials with the names of women who she believed were qualified for various government positions. Eleanor urged women to organize, campaign, and lobby when they felt strongly about a candidate or a cause.

No matter how much Franklin agreed with his wife's arguments for equality or how intelligently she could back her points up, his political advisers remained concerned. They did not think that citizens would support women's and civil rights. Regardless, the voice Eleanor gave to these issues won the Roosevelts the favor of women and African Americans. While Eleanor

Not a Popularity Contest

Despite the adoring, pleading letters that Eleanor received during her years in the White House, being First Lady was not always an easy—or popular—job. Whenever she spoke against segregation, certain members of the Southern press were eager to criticize her. If she demonstrated what women could accomplish in the workforce and society, the public accused her of overstepping her boundaries.

Franklin's presidential campaigns were yet another opportunity for people to comment on Eleanor, and their opinions were not always pleasant. During the 1940 election, Roosevelt opponents wore buttons saying "We don't want Eleanor either." Even her cousin Alice Roosevelt Longworth openly questioned why she was so involved in national affairs.

Eleanor, however, did not cease any of her social efforts or ask her husband to withdraw because of the criticism. Although she was distressed when she heard negative statements about her children, she accepted criticism— whether it was fair or not—as part of public life. At times, Eleanor was the most popular member of her family. In 1940, a poll revealed that 68 percent of Americans approved of her actions as First Lady. Franklin's approval rating was only 64 percent.

Religious Tolerance

As World War II broke out across Europe, Adolf Hitler's Nazi government increased its persecution of Jews. Eleanor took a stand against this discrimination—both at home and abroad. In 1937, Eleanor canceled a speech at a country club in Lancaster, Pennsylvania, when she discovered that it did not allow Jewish members. Eleanor also pleaded with government officials to accept more Jewish refugees. The United States refused entry to thousands of Jewish refugees during World War II.

championed reform, Franklin could take a more conservative approach to the issues.

THE POWER OF ONE WOMAN'S WORDS

The 1940 campaign brought its own share of challenges. While Franklin demonstrated that he could lead the country out of one disaster, another was brewing abroad. Europe and Asia had begun fighting World War II (1939–1945) the year before, and the United States had kept out of the conflict. As president, Franklin had to make sure that the United States was prepared for the possibility of war. By 1940, U.S. involvement seemed inevitable.

Eleanor later noted that she was not convinced her husband wanted to serve a third term in office. No other president had ever run for three terms. Eleanor remembered,

As time went on, more and more people came to me saying that he must run, that the threat of war was just over the

horizon and no one else had the prestige and the knowledge to carry on through a crisis. [4]

Still, Franklin had to convince the public—and members of his own political party—that he had made a wise decision in asking Henry Wallace to campaign for the vice presidency.

Democrats had mixed opinions about Wallace. His views were often considered radical or liberal. Conservative democrats were strongly opposed to Wallace. Many supporters wanted to nominate Franklin for another term, but his insistence on Wallace as a running mate angered them. Although Eleanor had previously chosen not to take an active role in her husband's campaigns, Franklin asked for her help at the Democratic National Convention of 1940.

On July 18, she spoke to the crowd gathered at Chicago Stadium in Chicago, Illinois:

> *… any man who is in an office of great responsibility today faces a heavier responsibility, perhaps, than any man has ever faced before in this country. … No man who is a candidate or who is President can carry this situation alone. This is only carried by a united people who love their country and who will live for it to the fullest of their ability … with a determination*

that their party shall be absolutely devoted to the good of the nation as a whole ... to bring the world to a safer and happier condition.[5]

Her brief speech moved the audience. She succeeded in calling for a strong, unified nation that could stand up against a world divided by war regardless of any controversy surrounding Eleanor's social beliefs or Franklin's running mate. In January 1941, Franklin began his third term as president, and the country waited anxiously as the possibility of war became more real. ‿

Last Minute

Eleanor did not rehearse her 1940 Democratic National Convention speech, but she did capture everyone's attention.

She later admitted, "I made up my mind that what I said would be brief. I had prepared nothing. ... The only way to accomplish my aim was to persuade the delegations in the convention to sink all personal interests in the interests of the country. ... While I spoke there was complete silence."[6]

Eleanor voiced her opinions through writing her "My Day" column and speaking at lectures and on the radio.

Eleanor meets with sailors in Bora Bora in 1943.

SEEING TO THE COUNTRY
AND SAYING GOOD-BYE

On December 7, 1941, any hopes that the United States had of staying out of World War II vanished. Japan, which was allied with Germany and Italy in the conflict, bombed the U.S. naval base in Pearl Harbor, Hawaii. Tensions had

been building between Japan and the United States
for some time. President Franklin Roosevelt declared
war, and the United States officially began fighting
alongside English, French, Chinese, and Soviet
troops.

Both Franklin's and Eleanor's responsibilities
increased immediately. Apart from official duties,
they had to put on a brave, patriotic face for the
nation. This was not an easy task in light of the
personal tragedy and stress they were
both experiencing. Earlier that year,
Franklin's mother and Eleanor's
brother Hall had died, and all four
of their sons had joined the military.
Neither Franklin nor the First
Lady had much time for personal
mourning or worrying. They needed
to help Americans prepare for the
sacrifices they would have to make.

Eleanor worked with the Office
of Civilian Defense (OCD). The
OCD was responsible for protecting
civilians, recruiting volunteers for
national defense, and keeping spirits
high during the conflict. Eleanor also

Mothers of Soldiers

With four sons enlisted
in the military, World
War II had a special
significance for Eleanor
that went beyond politics.
She felt the pain and wor-
ry of any parent whose
child was serving in the
war. Eleanor explained,
"During this second war
period I identified myself
with all the other women
who were going through
the same slow death,
and I kept praying that I
might be able to prevent a
repetition of the stupidity
called war."[1]

continued giving lectures, making radio broadcasts, and writing for various newspapers and magazines. She responded to letters written by soldiers and their families and frequently toured military hospitals. Her days were so full that she sometimes worked through the night. Plans had to be made, correspondence had to be read, and the country had to be cared for.

While it was one thing to address matters at home, Eleanor also made a point of traveling to countries where U.S. troops were stationed. She was saddened to see the loss and destruction caused by bombs when she traveled to England in 1942. As she later remembered,

> With the King and Queen I had my first real look at the devastation—blocks upon blocks of rubble. … One of the workers with whom I talked told me the hardest thing was to keep on at your job when you knew the bombs were falling in the area … and you did not know whether you would find your home and family still there at the end of your day's or night's work.[2]

Eleanor was inspired by the determination and hope of people in countries that had been completely torn apart by violence and chaos. She was also mindful of the many American soldiers and volunteers who were far away from their loved ones while they served overseas. Once Eleanor returned to Washington, D.C., she wrote to the relieved and grateful relatives of the U.S. troops she had visited abroad to let them know she had seen their family members.

Her 1942 tour of England would not be the last time the First Lady brought comfort to American soldiers away from home. In 1943, Eleanor traveled to islands in the South Pacific, another dangerous location during the war. She was clearly courageous and dedicated to the troops. Yet she recognized that other causes also demanded her attention. Discrimination and women's rights issues had existed long before World War II and now needed to be addressed more seriously than ever.

Visiting Soldiers

When Eleanor visited wounded soldiers in military hospitals in the South Pacific, she was more concerned about cheering up the troops than her own comfort. She saw hospitals that were plagued by snakes, rats, and insects. Sometimes patients recognized her from her travels across the United States during the Great Depression. Many soldiers were pleased to hear that Eleanor remembered having visited their hometowns.

Battles Waged in Washington, D.C.

Eleanor had a history of fighting discrimination, which she felt destroyed the spirit and unity that made the United States so unique. As the war continued, it was clear that the nation could not afford to be divided or to hold back talented, hard-working citizens based on gender or skin color.

With many men serving in the military, the jobs that people had fought so desperately to find during the Great Depression were suddenly abandoned. The war created a demand for military supplies and weapons. Factories reopened and laborers were needed to help mass-produce these items. Women seized the opportunity to enter the workforce and serve their country. Eleanor wanted to make sure they were treated fairly.

Most women not only spent long hours at their jobs but also had to cook and clean when they got home. Some women who wanted to work

Women in the Workforce

Approximately 6 million women held down jobs in factories while World War II raged overseas. Many people assumed that when the troops returned home, they would simply pick up where they had left off. Approximately 80 percent of women, however, preferred to continue working. Eleanor supported their efforts and advised that all people who wanted to work should be allowed to do so. However, many of the women who continued to work were forced to take jobs that were considered more appropriate for women.

could not because they had no one to watch their children during the day. These women needed to be employed in order to support their families. No one knew when the war would end or if their husbands would return. Eleanor encouraged factory owners and business managers to offer on-site daycare for working mothers. She also fought for better wages for the United States' new female labor force. In her mind, women deserved the same pay as men if they were going to do the same amount of work.

Eleanor fought just as hard for the rights of African Americans. Just as she had praised the skills of the Tuskegee Airmen to Franklin, she also encouraged him to sign an order in 1941 prohibiting discrimination in the defense industry. The order called for the creation of a committee to investigate complaints by workers who felt they were being treated unfairly. These measures opened up new employment opportunities for African Americans across the country.

Eleanor recognized that African-American women faced a doubly difficult challenge due to their race and gender. Because the Army Nurse Corps was reluctant to accept non-white nurses, many African-American nurses were turned away. Thanks in part to Eleanor's urging, as World War II progressed, African-American nurses were recruited in greater numbers.

Japanese Internment

After Pearl Harbor, the U.S. government feared another Japanese attack along the United States' West Coast. President Roosevelt authorized the removal of anyone of Japanese ancestry in this area to internment camps known as "War Relocation Centers." Approximately 110,000 people from California and parts of Arizona, Washington, and Oregon were relocated to these camps. These camps were unconstitutional and violated Japanese-Americans' civil rights.

Many historians believe that Eleanor opposed the relocation efforts, which often separated families and caused people to lose their jobs, belongings, and sense of identity. She encouraged Americans not to discriminate against the Japanese who were released from the camps. As she wrote in *Collier's Magazine* in October 1943:

... it is to your advantage ... to try to regard them as individuals and not to condemn them before they are given a fair chance to prove themselves in the community. ... Every citizen in this country has a right to our basic freedoms ... and we retain the right to lead our individual lives as we please, but we can only do so if we grant to others the freedoms that we wish for ourselves.[4]

FINAL DAYS AS FIRST LADY

In 1944, the conflict continued. Franklin successfully campaigned for a fourth term of office—this time asking Harry S. Truman to be his running mate. As Eleanor recalled, "I knew without asking that as long as the war was on ... that Franklin, if he was well enough, would run again."[3]

In January 1945, all 13 of the

Roosevelts' grandchildren visited the White House at about the time Franklin was preparing for his fourth inauguration. The president, like most Americans, sensed that peace was near and that the United States would likely claim victory in the war. Franklin was aware that his health was failing. He also understood that the end of the war would not necessarily mean the end of conflict. He was concerned about future relationships with the Soviet Union and the unrest in the Middle East. There was still much to be done. However, it was becoming clear that the time Franklin had left was limited.

On April 12, Eleanor attended a benefit while Franklin was at Warm Springs, Georgia, where he had received therapy since becoming paralyzed. That day, he fainted while posing for a portrait. As the hours passed, he worsened. Eleanor received a call telling her to return home. Eleanor sat stiffly in the car back to the White House. She was certain of what was coming. It was not long before she was informed that Franklin had died of a brain hemorrhage.

For Eleanor, her family, and the entire country, the next few days were filled with tremendous sorrow. But there was also evidence of the enormous respect Americans had for their leader. As the train carried the First Lady and her husband's body back to Washington, D.C., people came out all through the night to pay their respects to the president. Franklin was buried in the rose garden at his family's estate in Hyde Park on April 15.

Eleanor immediately prepared to move out of the White House. Truman would take over the heavy responsibilities as president of a nation that was still at war. She later noted,

> *I felt I wanted to leave it as soon as possible. I had already started to prepare directions so that the accumulation of twelve years could be quickly packed and shipped. As always happens in life, something was coming to an end and something new was beginning.*[5]

President Truman

Eleanor felt very sorry for Truman after her husband's death. As president, Truman did not have an easy task ahead of him. His job was made more difficult by the fact that he had seen very little of Franklin during his brief term as vice president.

The two men had shared few discussions about peace efforts or future conflicts. As Truman later recollected, "I felt like the moon, the stars, and all the planets had fallen on me."[6]

Truman eventually made the decision to drop the atomic bomb on Hiroshima and Nagasaki in Japan. Though the bombs caused devastating damage, they helped expedite the end of the war.

Franklin was buried in Hyde Park on April 15, 1945.

United Nations delegates Sucheta Kirpalani, Barbara Castle, Carrie R. Wilson, and Eleanor Roosevelt meet before General Assembly.

New Beginnings, Countless Nations

fter Franklin's death, Eleanor was somewhat uncertain about her future. She continued her writing, public lectures, and radio broadcasts in order to earn an income. As she later recalled this time in her life, she explained,

I had few definite plans but there were certain things I did not want to do. I did not want to run an elaborate household again. I did not want to cease trying to be useful in some way.[1]

It was not hard for Eleanor to fulfill these wishes. She moved back to New York and, in December of 1945, she accepted an appointment from President Truman as a delegate to the United Nations (UN). The UN had been created only two months earlier and included representatives from 50 nations. These representatives were responsible for working together to promote international peace, security, and economic progress. Eleanor took her new job seriously, and she quickly earned a reputation for her hard work and dedication.

As a delegate, Eleanor played a role in drafting the Universal Declaration of Human Rights, which was adopted by the UN in December 1948. The declaration proclaimed the essential rights guaranteed to all people. These included the rights to life, liberty, an education, and

Author

Eleanor earned a portion of her income by writing books. Twenty-eight titles were published between 1932 and 1963. These books included autobiographical information, political essays, and even advice regarding good table manners. As with her public speeches and social efforts, Eleanor used her abilities as an author to honestly address issues that she considered worthwhile.

freedom of thought and expression. Eleanor believed that a common understanding of human rights was important in establishing peace.

Social and Political

During her years at the White House, Eleanor poured tea and hosted dinner parties. More importantly, she served on several committees and worked with government organizations.

Her exposure to both social and political settings proved valuable during her time with the UN. As she later noted, "I established a custom ... throughout the years I was connected with the United Nations, of trying to get together with other nations' representatives at luncheon or dinner or for a few hours in the eve-ning. I found that often a few people of different nationalities, meeting on a semi-social basis, could talk together about a common problem with better results than when they were meeting offi-cially as a committee."[2]

OUTSPOKEN AS EVER

Despite Eleanor's contributions to the international community, not every president who followed in Franklin's footsteps appreciated her bold opinions. Most respected her and sought her political support, but a few tried to limit her voice in their administrations. Dwight D. Eisenhower, who served from 1953 to 1961, asked Eleanor to resign as a delegate to the UN shortly after he was elected president. Eleanor agreed, though she did not abandon her work for human rights.

Even though World War II had officially ended in 1945, tension continued to exist between several nations. Just as she had visited combat zones in the early 1940s, Eleanor was similarly unafraid to

General Dwight Eisenhower meets with Eleanor Roosevelt in Hyde Park.

venture into areas that were filled with bloodshed
or hostility in the 1950s. Between 1952 and 1957,
she traveled to countries such as Lebanon, Jordan,
India, Israel, Nepal, Indonesia, Chile, the Soviet
Union, Japan, Greece, Morocco, and Iran. She

met with political leaders to learn about different national governments and encourage them to promote peace and social progress.

Eleanor also used these travels as a chance to give lectures and continue writing books and articles. As she made her way around the globe, Eleanor concluded:

We have to show the world by our actions that we live up to the ideals we profess and demonstrate that we can provide all the people in this country with the basic decencies of life, spiritually as well as materially.[4]

A Painful Reminder of the Need for Peace

During her 1953 trip to Japan, Eleanor visited Hiroshima, where the United States dropped an atomic bomb in August 1945. The nuclear attack and its aftereffects killed approximately 140,000 people and caused widespread devastation. Japan surrendered in World War II less than a month later.

In 1958, Eleanor recognized that the destruction created by the bomb touched people all across the world. She realized how pointless it was to lay blame on one particular side, country, or individual in the face of so many wasted lives. As she said,

It is useless to say that Germany started the war. ... It is useless to remember, as I did, the feelings of my husband and of the people of the United States when he heard the shocking news of the Japanese attack on Pearl Harbor. ... It was not just here in this sad Japanese city that men and women and children suffered. All the world suffered. So it seems to me that the only helpful thing we can do ... is to pledge ourselves to ... eliminate the causes of war through ... the machinery of the United Nations. ... Contemplating the fate of Hiroshima, one can only say: "God grant to men greater wisdom in the future."[3]

She recognized that for other nations to look upon the United States as a role model, U.S. citizens had to correct issues such as discrimination and poverty. Eleanor resumed her fight for the causes she had always held dear. She also began championing a few new ones. She pushed for equal education for African Americans, supported female political candidates, and urged officials to increase the minimum wage paid to laborers.

During the 1940s and 1950s, the country was in the midst of the Cold War. Tension was growing between the democratic United States and the communist Soviet Union. Americans feared Communism, seeing it as a threat to their way of life. During what became known as the Red Scare, people were frequently accused—often with no proof—of being disloyal or un-American if they questioned the U.S. government. Because of her social activism and her belief that the United States would benefit from growth and change, some leaders questioned her

Dedication to Civil Rights

As First Lady, Eleanor received some heated criticism from Southern newspapers for her fight against discrimination. In 1958, the Ku Klux Klan (KKK)—a racist organization that often violently attacked African Americans and others— offered a $25,000 reward for her capture. Eleanor was 74 years old at the time and no longer had U.S. Secret Service protection. Not surprisingly, this did not keep her from attending civil-rights workshops in the South and continuing her other efforts to end segregation.

Eleanor advised President John F. Kennedy on his campaign.

patriotism. Senator Joseph McCarthy and Federal
Bureau of Investigation (FBI) Director J. Edgar
Hoover suspected she supported Communism.

As Eleanor wrote in her "My Day" column,

> All of these attitudes are attitudes of fear. They show lack
> of confidence in ourselves and in others. For the leading
> democracy in the world to indulge in them is a very great
> danger, not to us alone but also to the world.[5]

She strongly opposed any efforts that made Americans afraid to voice their opinions or to improve society. Eleanor was not concerned about impressing men such as Hoover and McCarthy. By 1960, she was 76 years old and had already proven her dedication to her country and its people.

A GLOW THAT WARMED THE WORLD

After leaving the White House, Eleanor demonstrated that she did not need the title of First Lady to serve the nation. In fact, many continued to seek her voice and support. Political candidates and future presidents John F. Kennedy and Lyndon B. Johnson asked for her help in their campaigns for the Democratic nomination in 1960. Kennedy visited Eleanor at Hyde Park, where she advised him to focus on civil rights. According to Eleanor, Kennedy would need the support of African Americans in the election. Kennedy had no hope of winning the South without the support of African Americans. Her presence and opinions were sought by everyone from university heads to television producers.

Eleanor died on November 7, 1962, from health problems related to tuberculosis. President

Kennedy and former presidents Truman and Eisenhower attended her funeral, as did political leaders, social activists, colleagues, friends, and family members. She was buried next to Franklin's grave in Hyde Park. People mourned a great loss while remembering an even greater lady.

Eleanor experienced several personal and public challenges, but she worked through her struggles and always tried to learn from them. When she saw the need for change, she believed it was worth fighting for. As Eleanor once said,

> ... it is more intelligent to hope rather than to fear, to try rather than not to try. For one thing we know beyond all doubt: Nothing has ever been achieved by the person who says, "It can't be done."[6]

Obituary

On November 8, 1962, the *New York Times* printed an obituary about how Eleanor would be remembered in history: "She had become not only the wife and widow of a towering President but a noble personality in herself. In the White House and for some time thereafter, no First Lady could touch Mrs. Roosevelt for causes espoused, opinions expressed, distances spanned, people spoken to, words printed, precedents shattered, honors conferred, degrees garnered."[7]

Eleanor Roosevelt, 1957

TIMELINE

1884	1899	1903
Anna Eleanor Roosevelt is born in New York City on October 11.	Eleanor enrolls at Allenswood School outside of London, where she meets her mentor, Mademoiselle Marie Souvestre.	Eleanor joins the Junior League and volunteers amidst the slums on New York's Lower East Side.

1921	1922	1928
Franklin is diagnosed with polio in August; Eleanor cares for him and encourages him not to give up his political career.	Eleanor joins the Women's Trade Union League and the Women's Division of the Democratic State Committee.	Eleanor attends the Democratic National Convention in June; party leaders ask her to convince Franklin to run for governor of New York.

1905

Eleanor marries Franklin Delano Roosevelt on March 17.

1917

The United States enters World War I on April 6. Eleanor volunteers with the Red Cross and helps found the Navy Red Cross.

1919

Eleanor attends the first International Congress of Working Women in Washington, D.C., on October 28.

1932

Franklin is elected president on November 8; he takes office on March 4, 1933.

1933

Construction begins on the Arthurdale Subsistence Homestead Project in West Virginia; Eleanor actively supports New Deal programs.

1935

The National Youth Administration is authorized as a New Deal program on June 26.

TIMELINE

1935

Eleanor begins writing her "My Day" column on December 30.

1939

Eleanor resigns her membership with the Daughters of the American Revolution on February 26.

1940

Eleanor gives a speech at the Democratic National Convention in Chicago; Franklin is nominated for a third presidential term.

1943

Eleanor visits U.S. troops on 17 South Pacific islands, New Zealand, and Australia.

1945

Franklin dies of a hemorrhage on April 12; Eleanor leaves the White House and returns to New York.

1945

Eleanor accepts appointment as a delegate to the United Nations in December and holds this position until August 1953.

1941	1941	1942
Eleanor flies over Tuskegee Army Air Field with African-American flight instructor Charles A. Anderson on April 19.	The Japanese attack Pearl Harbor on December 7; the United States officially enters World War II one day later.	Eleanor begins a three-week tour of war-torn England on October 23.

1952	1960	1962
Eleanor begins traveling to foreign nations, where she gives lectures, meets with leaders, and promotes peace and human rights.	Eleanor lends her public support to presidential candidate John F. Kennedy.	Eleanor dies on November 7 at the age of 78; she is buried next to Franklin in Hyde Park.

ESSENTIAL FACTS

DATE OF BIRTH

October 11, 1884

PLACE OF BIRTH

New York City, New York

DATE OF DEATH

November 7, 1962

PARENTS

Elliott Roosevelt and Anna Hall

EDUCATION

Allenswood School, England

MARRIAGE

Franklin Delano Roosevelt (March 17, 1905)

CHILDREN

Anna, James, Franklin Jr. (died at eight months), Elliott, Franklin Jr., and John

CAREER HIGHLIGHTS

In December 1935, Eleanor started writing her own newspaper column "My Day." She used this column to comment on everything from political issues to performances in the theatre. After Franklin's death, Eleanor was selected in December 1945 as a delegate to the United Nations, where she helped draft the Universal Declaration of Human Rights.

Societal Contribution

Eleanor volunteered for various public service causes throughout her life, including volunteering with the Red Cross during World War I. She also publicly fought against discrimination by race or gender. She supported the Women's Suffrage Movement.

Residences

Hyde Park, New York; Albany, New York; Washington, D.C.; Campobello Island, New Brunswick, Canada

Public Conflicts

Eleanor was criticized for overstepping her bounds as First Lady and having too much influence over the president. Her views concerning poverty and women's and civil rights were often considered controversial.

Personal Conflicts

Eleanor lost both of her parents and her brother Elliott Jr. when she was a young girl. She moved in with her strict Grandmother Hall and was insecure and shy while growing up. Eleanor's mother-in-law, Sara Delano Roosevelt, was often overbearing and difficult for Eleanor to deal with. In 1918, Eleanor discovered that her husband, Franklin, was having an affair with her secretary. Franklin ended the relationship, and he and Eleanor remained married.

Quote

"Do what you feel in your heart to be right—for you'll be criticized anyway. You'll be damned if you do, and damned if you don't."

—*Eleanor Roosevelt*

ADDITIONAL RESOURCES

SELECT BIBLIOGRAPHY

Black, Allida M., ed. *What I Hope to Leave Behind: The Essential Essays of Eleanor Roosevelt*. Brooklyn, NY: Carlson Publishing Company, 1995.

Emblidge, David, ed. *Eleanor Roosevelt's My Day*. New York: Pharos Books, 1990.

Hickok, Lorena A. *Eleanor Roosevelt: Reluctant First Lady*. New York: Dodd, Mead & Company, 1962.

Knepper, Cathy, ed. *Dear Mrs. Roosevelt: Letters to Eleanor Roosevelt Through Depression and War*. New York: Carroll & Graf Publishers, 2004.

Roosevelt, Eleanor. *The Autobiography of Eleanor Roosevelt*. New York: Da Capo Press, 1992.

FURTHER READING

Fleming, Candace. *Our Eleanor: A Scrapbook Look at Eleanor Roosevelt's Remarkable Life*. New York: Atheneum Books for Young Readers, 2005.

Jones, Victoria Garrett. *Eleanor Roosevelt: A Courageous Spirit*. New York: Sterling Publishing Company, 2007.

Rosenberg, Pam. *Eleanor Roosevelt: First Lady, Humanitarian, and World Citizen*. Chanhassen, MN: The Child's World, 2004.

Somervill, Barbara A. *Eleanor Roosevelt: First Lady of the World*. Minneapolis, MN: Compass Point Books, 2006.

Trumbauer, Lisa. *Eleanor Roosevelt*. Mankato, MN: Capstone Press, 2005.

Web Links

To learn more about Eleanor Roosevelt, visit ABDO Publishing Company on the World Wide Web at **www.abdopublishing.com**. Web sites about Eleanor Roosevelt are featured on our Book Links page. These links are routinely monitored and updated to provide the most current information available.

Places to Visit

Eleanor Roosevelt National Historic Site
4097 Albany Post Road, Hyde Park, NY 12538
800-337-8474
www.nps.gov/elro/
Visit Val-Kil cottage, where Eleanor began a small furniture business.

Roosevelt Campobello International Park
459 Route 774, Welshpool, Campobello Island, New Brunswick, Canada E5E 1A4
506-752-2922
www.nps.gov/roca/
Campobello Island was the Roosevelts' favorite vacation spot. It currently serves as a memorial to FDR.

The White House
1600 Pennsylvania Avenue NW, Washington, DC 20500
202-456-7041
www.whitehouse.gov/history/tours/
White House tours offer visitors a historic look into past presidencies.

GLOSSARY

ambassador
An official representative from one country to another.

canteen
A recreation area where soldiers can eat, drink, and socialize.

communism
A political system in which the government controls the economy and property is shared and owned by the community.

defense industry
Businesses that work with the government to produce military supplies and equipment.

delegate
Someone appointed to act as a representative.

democracy
A government in which citizens exercise power by voting and electing leaders to represent them.

diphtheria
A throat disease that often causes a high fever and difficulty breathing.

diplomat
An individual who officially represents his or her government in a foreign country and who helps maintain international relations.

headmistress
The chief female teacher who manages a boarding school.

hemorrhage
Heavy bleeding that can occur on either the inside or outside of a person's body.

inauguration
A swearing-in ceremony.

influenza
An infection affecting the nose, throat, and lungs that is also commonly referred to as the "flu."

lynch
> To kill a person (often by hanging) without the authority of the law.

matron
> A woman who is married and has children.

morphine
> A powerful and often addictive drug used to relieve pain.

philanthropist
> A person who uses his or her time and money to help others.

polio
> An infectious, contagious disease that can affect a person's nervous system and cause paralysis.

refugee
> A person who flees his or her country because it is unsafe or because he or she is suffering from persecution.

scarlet fever
> A childhood infection involving fever and a red rash.

segregation
> Separate treatment or opportunities given to people based on their gender, religion, or race.

stock market
> The organized buying and selling of shares of ownership in businesses and corporations.

sweatshop
> A factory where laborers usually work long hours in unsafe or uncomfortable conditions and generally earn little pay.

tenement house
> A run-down apartment that often provides residents with limited safety, comfort, and basic necessities.

tuberculosis
> An infection that affects a person's lungs.

Source Notes

Chapter 1. Flight at Tuskegee
1. *History 313: The History of African Americans in the West.* 13 Dec. 2006. University of Washington Department of History. 31 Jan. 2007 <http://faculty.washington.edu/qtaylor/Courses/313_AAW/313_manual_cp_08.htm>.
2. Cathy D. Knepper, ed. *Dear Mrs. Roosevelt.* New York: Carroll & Graf Publishers, 2004. 195.
3. Ibid. 195–196.
4. *State of Oregon Department of Human Services.* 23 June 2006. Official Oregon State Web Site. 31 Jan. 2007 <http://www.oregon.gov/DHS/news/messages/2006messages/2006-0623.shtml>.

Chapter 2. A Childhood Filled with Challenges
1. Eleanor Roosevelt. *The Autobiography of Eleanor Roosevelt.* New York: Harper & Brothers, 1961. 5.
2. Ibid. 17.
3. Ibid.
4. Ibid. 11.
5. Ibid. 15.

Chapter 3. Eager for Social Change
1. Eleanor Roosevelt. *The Autobiography of Eleanor Roosevelt.* New York: Harper & Brothers, 1961. 29–30.
2. Ibid. 27.
3. Eleanor Roosevelt Quotes. *The Quotations Page.* 1994–2007. <http://www.quotationspage.com/quotes/Eleanor_Roosevelt>.
4. Eleanor Roosevelt. *The Autobiography of Eleanor Roosevelt.* New York: Harper & Brothers, 1961. 40.

Chapter 4. Starting a Family

1. Eleanor Roosevelt. *The Autobiography of Eleanor Roosevelt.* New York: Harper & Brothers, 1961. 41.
2. *Newspaper Article on Eleanor Roosevelt's Wedding.* 6 Apr. 2004. National Park Service: Eleanor Roosevelt National Historic Site. 16 Feb. 2007 <http://www.nps.gov/archive/elro/who-is-er/q-and-a/q8-newsarticle.htm>.
3. Eleanor Roosevelt. *The Autobiography of Eleanor Roosevelt.* New York: Harper & Brothers, 1961. 50.
4. Ibid. 61.
5. Ibid.

Chapter 5. More Than a Politician's Wife

1. Eleanor Roosevelt. *The Autobiography of Eleanor Roosevelt.* New York: Harper & Brothers, 1961. 83.
2. Ibid. 93.
3. Ibid. 68.
4. Ibid. 113.

Chapter 6. Paving the Way to the White House

1. Eleanor Roosevelt. *The Autobiography of Eleanor Roosevelt.* New York: Harper & Brothers, 1961. 161–162.
2. Ibid. 163.
3. Ibid. 168.
4. Cathy D. Knepper, ed. *Dear Mrs. Roosevelt.* New York: Carroll & Graf Publishers, 2004. 16.
5. Ibid. 30.
6. Ibid. 7.
7. Eleanor Roosevelt. *The Autobiography of Eleanor Roosevelt.* New York: Harper & Brothers, 1961. 130.

Source Notes Continued

Chapter 7. Unafraid to Make Waves

1. *American Originals—Eleanor Roosevelt's Letter of Resignation to the DAR.*
Mar. 1996. National Archives and Records Administration. 21
Feb. 2007 <http://www.archives.gov/exhibits/american_originals/
eleanor.html>.
2. Eleanor Roosevelt. *The Autobiography of Eleanor Roosevelt.* New York:
Harper & Brothers, 1961. 191.
3. Ibid. 193.
4. Ibid. 214.
5. *Address to the 1940 Democratic Convention.* 4 Jan. 2006. The Eleanor
Roosevelt Papers Project at George Washington University. 21 Feb.
2007 <http://www.gwu.edu/~erpapers/teachinger/q-and-a/q22-
erspeech.cfm>.
6. Eleanor Roosevelt. *The Autobiography of Eleanor Roosevelt.* New York:
Harper & Brothers, 1961. 217.

Chapter 8. Seeing to the Country and Saying Good-bye

1. Eleanor Roosevelt. *The Autobiography of Eleanor Roosevelt.* New York:
Harper & Brothers, 1961. 251.
2. Ibid. 243–244.
3. Ibid. 269.
4. *A Challenge to American Sportsmanship.* 4 Jan. 2006. The Eleanor
Roosevelt Papers Project at George Washington University. 23
Feb. 2007 <http://www.gwu.edu/~erpapers/documents/articles/
challengetoamerican.cfm>.
5. Eleanor Roosevelt. *The Autobiography of Eleanor Roosevelt.* New York:
Harper & Brothers, 1961. 277.
6. *Harry S. Truman.* The White House. 23 Feb. 2007 <http://www.
whitehouse.gov/history/presidents/ht33.html>.

Chapter 9. New Beginnings, Countless Nations

1. Eleanor Roosevelt. *The Autobiography of Eleanor Roosevelt.* New York: Harper & Brothers, 1961. 283–284.

2. Ibid. 385.

3. David Emblidge, ed. *Eleanor Roosevelt's My Day—Volume II: The Post-War Years.* New York: Pharos Books, 1990. 95.

4. *Quotations by Eleanor Roosevelt.* 4 Jan. 2006. The Eleanor Roosevelt Papers Project at George Washington University. 25 Feb. 2007 <http://www.gwu.edu/~erpapers/abouteleanor/er-quotes/>.

5. Ibid. 340–341.

6. Ibid. 305.

7. "Mrs. Roosevelt Dies at 78 After Illness of Six Weeks." 1996. *The New York Times Magazine*: Heroine Worship. 23 Feb. 2007 <http://www.nytimes.com/specials/magazine4/toc.html>.

INDEX

ABOUT THE AUTHOR

Katie Marsico writes children's books from her home near Chicago, Illinois. She lives with her husband and their two children. Before beginning her career as an author, Marsico worked as a managing editor in children's publishing. She dedicates this book to her mother and husband, who have always supported her and who continue to inspire her.

PHOTO CREDITS

Courtesy of the Franklin D. Roosevelt Library & Museum, cover, 3, 6, 14, 17, 19, 23, 24, 28, 34, 40, 43, 44, 48, 53, 54, 60, 62, 66, 75, 76, 85, 89, 95, 96, 97, 98, 99; Library of Congress, 9, 33; National Air and Space Museum, Smithsonian Institution (SI 90-7010), 13; AP Images, 38, 65, 86, 92.